FORCE & MOTION

by Clint Twist

Consultants: Linda McGuigan and Professor Terry Russell
Center for Research in Primary Science and Technology, University of Liverpool

Library of Congress Cataloging-in-Publication Data

Twist, Clint.
   Force & Motion / by Clint Twist.
      p. cm. — (Check it out!)
   Includes index.
   ISBN 1-59716-061-X (library binding) — ISBN 1-59716-098-9 (pbk.)
   1. Force and energy—Juvenile literature. 2. Motion—Juvenile literature.
   I. Title: Force and Motion. II. Title. III. Series.

   QC73.4T85 2006
   531'.6—dc22

2005009763

For more information, write to Bearport Publishing Company, Inc., 101 Fifth Avenue, Suite 6R, New York, New York 10003. Printed in the United States of America.

1 2 3 4 5 6 7 8 9 10

Contents

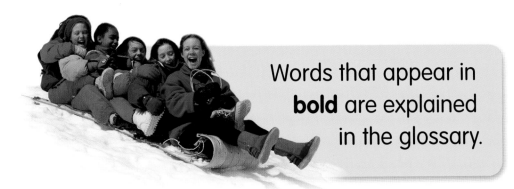

Words that appear in **bold** are explained in the glossary.

Motion

When things are moving, they are in **motion**.
Things in motion move from one **position**
to another.

The tiger is walking
across the snow.
He is in motion.
Walking and
running are both
types of motion.

Motion = A change in
position

What do you think?

...ings that are not moving are
...t in motion. Their positions
...o not change.

No motion

The tiger has stopped moving.
What happens to the tiger's
position when he is not in motion?

(Answer on page 20)

5

Pushing

A **force** is something that causes motion.
Pushing is one kind of force.

This cat is pushing the wagon. She is using force to make the wagon move.

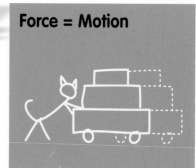

Force = Motion

What do you think?

When two cats push against the wagon, more force is used.

More force

Will two cats move the wagon more than one cat?

(Answer on page 20)

7

Pulling

Pulling is another type of force.

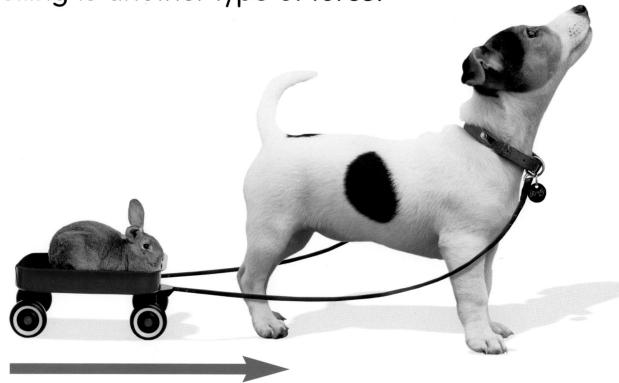

It is easy to pull something light.
You do not need to use much force.
This dog can easily pull one small rabbit.

Something light = Less
force needed to pull

What do you think?

It is harder to pull something that is heavy.

Something heavy

Will the dog use more force to pull many rabbits than he used to pull just one rabbit?

(Answer on page 20)

Changes in Motion

Objects do not all move at the same **speed**. The more force you use to move an object, the faster it will move.

A marble moves quickly when the player uses a lot of force to flick it.

More force = Faster speed

What do you think?

A strong push will make this car move quickly.

Less force

How do you think this boy can make his car move slowly?

(Answer on page 20)

11

Slopes

Slopes change how much force is needed to move something. It takes less force to move something down a slope.

It is easy for this bear to slide down the hill.

Down = Less force needed

What do you think?

These dogs are pulling a sled up a slope.

Up

Will the dogs use more force
going up or down a slope?

(Answer on page 21)

13

Friction

Friction is a force that stops things from moving easily. Friction happens when things slide against one another. **Smooth** surfaces cause less friction than **rough** ones.

Snow is smooth. Things can slide easily on snow.

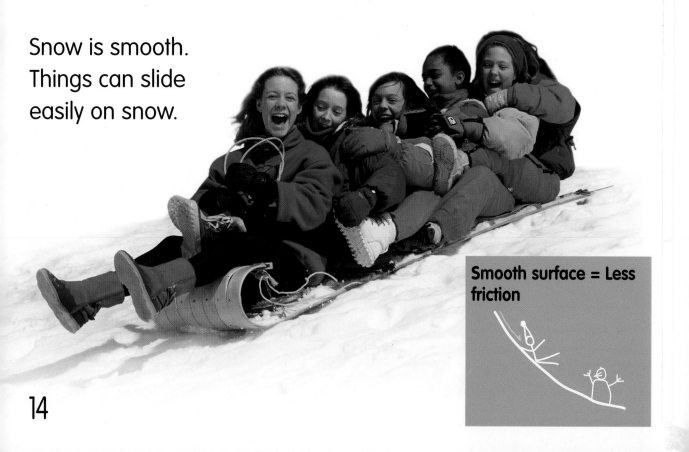

Smooth surface = Less friction

What do you think?

Grass has a rougher surface than snow.

Is it harder to slide down a snowy or grassy slope?

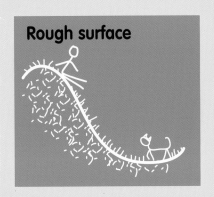

(Answer on page 21)

Changing Shape

Force doesn't just make things move.
Force can also change the shape of some
objects. The more force you use, the more
the shape will change.

You can push
and pull dough
into shapes with
your hands.

Small force = Shape
changes
a little.

16

What do you think?

When you push your finger gently against a piece of clay, you can change its shape a little.

More force

What will happen to the shape of the clay if you push with more force?

(Answer on page 21)

17

Changing Direction

Force can be used to change the **direction** of a moving object.

When the boy kicks the ball, he's using force to move it. He pushes the ball in a direction.

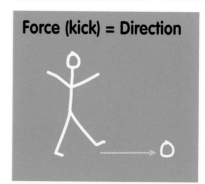

Force (kick) = Direction

What do you think?

Another soccer player tries to change the direction of a ball by using force.

Added force

What happens to the direction of the ball when the player kicks it?

(Answer on page 21) 19

Answers

Page 5

The tiger's position stays the same when he is not in motion.

No motion = Position stays the same

Page 7

Two cats will move the wagon more than one cat.

More force = More motion

Page 9

The dog will use more force to pull many rabbits than he used to pull one rabbit.

Something heavy = More force needed to pull

Page 11

The car will move slowly if the boy pushes it with less force.

Less force = Slower speed

Page 13

The dogs will use more force going up a slope.

Up = More force needed

Page 15

It is harder to slide down a grassy slope because there is more friction.

Rough surface = More friction

Page 17

Using more force will change the shape of the clay more.

More force = Shape changes more

Page 19

The direction of the ball changes when the player kicks it.

Added force = Direction may change

Glossary

direction
(duh-REK-shuhn)
the way that something
is moving

force (FORSS)
something that causes
movement, such as a
pull or push

friction (FRIK-shuhn)
a force that slows down
objects that are rubbing
against each other

motion
(MOH-shuhn)
another word for
movement

position
(puh-ZISH-uhn)
the place where
an object is

rough (RUHF)
describes a surface
with many bumps

slopes (SLOHPS) lines or surfaces with one end higher than the other

speed (SPEED) the rate at which an object moves over a distance

smooth (SMOOTH) describes a surface that has no bumps

23

Index

Picture credits

Corbis: 4, 5, 12, 13.
Powerstock: front cover, 1, 2, 3, 6, 7, 8, 9, 10, 11, 14, 15, 16, 17, 18, 19, 23, 24.

Every effort has been made to trace the copyright holders, and we apologize in advance for any unintentional omissions. We would be pleased to insert the appropriate acknowledgments in any subsequent edition of this publication.